Many Kinds of Homes

by Nancy Craig

Editorial Offices: Glenview, Illinois • Parsippany, New Jersey • New York, New York
Sales Offices: Needham, Massachusetts • Duluth, Georgia • Glenview, Illinois
Coppell, Texas • Sacramento, California • Mesa, Arizona

Some regions of America were covered with trees.

The United States has different regions, or areas. Each region has a different climate and resources. Some of those resources are wood, grass, soil, and clay. In the past, Americans used the resources of their region to build homes.

Many people from Europe came to the eastern part of North America. They found land that was covered with trees. There was plenty of wood.

---

climate: kind of weather

resources: supplies that people need

log cabin

Early English settlers lived in houses made of wood, like this one.

What do you think many people used to build homes?

The settlers cut down some of the trees. They cleared the land to build wooden houses. As time passed, they learned more about the climate and made some changes to their homes. They built bigger fireplaces to heat their homes in winter. They dug cellars to keep their food cool so it would not spoil in the warm summer.

---

settlers: people who settle in a new land

The plains were covered with tall grass.

Pioneers moved west. There were not many trees on the plains. Instead there were miles and miles of grasslands. The pioneers couldn't build wooden homes. They needed a new idea.

What do you think the pioneers used to build their homes?

---

pioneers: people who settle in a new place
plains: flat areas of land

The pioneers made homes from the grassy soil. They cut blocks of sod out of the earth. They used the sod blocks like bricks. They stacked up the sod blocks to build walls.

These sod houses were called *soddies.* The thick grass-and-dirt bricks kept out cold air in the winter. They kept out hot air in the summer. But soddies were not permanent homes. When the settlers could afford to buy wood from other places, they built wooden homes.

sod house

---
sod: soil with grass and roots attached

This pueblo was built long ago.

Another group of people, Native Americans called the Pueblo people, live in the American Southwest. The climate there is hot and dry, and there are few trees. The Pueblo people began building their pueblos, or villages, long ago. There was not much wood, but they had clay in the ground.

What do you think Pueblo people used to build homes long ago?

This is a pueblo today.

The Pueblo people used what they had. They mixed clay with water. They shaped the clay into bricks called *adobe bricks*.

Then they used the bricks to build tall, steep buildings. Today, there are tall and not-very-tall pueblos. Some look like apartments.

For much of the year, Inuit land is covered with snow.

The Inuit people live in Alaska. Most of the year, the land where many Inuit live is covered with snow. Today, the Inuit live in modern homes like those in other parts of the United States. In the past, they built homes from sod.

But also in the past, the Inuit people did not always spend the whole year in one place. When they traveled, they could not take their homes with them.

Where do you think the Inuit people lived when they traveled?

igloo

    In summer, the travelers used tents made from animal skins. The tents were not warm enough for the cold winters, though.
    Winter travelers used snow to build shelters called *igloos*. The Inuit people had long knives made from animal bones. They cut big blocks of snow with the knives. Then they stacked the blocks on top of each other. A small fire in the igloo kept it warm. A hole let the smoke escape.

Brick homes are everywhere.

Today building materials are shipped all over the country. Builders no longer need to use nearby resources. They can build any kind of home in any region.

Many homes are still made of wood.

Some homes have lots of glass.

Homes can be made of metal.

log home

Some new homes look like homes from the past. Builders still build log cabins. Some builders use adobe bricks. Some build apartment buildings that look something like pueblos.

What clues show that the log home in this picture is new?